BABY BLUES® **14** SCRAPBOOK

MOTHERHOOD
IS NOT FOR WIMPS

Other Baby Blues® books from Andrews McMeel Publishing

Guess Who Didn't Take a Nap?
I Thought Labor Ended When the Baby Was Born
We Are Experiencing Parental Difficulties... Please Stand By
Night of the Living Dad
I Saw Elvis in My Ultrasound
One More and We're Outnumbered!
Check, Please...
threats, bribes & videotape
If I'm a Stay-At-Home Mom, Why Am I Always in the Car?
Lift and Separate
I Shouldn't Have to Scream More Than Once!

Treasuries

The Super-Absorbent Biodegradable Family-Size Baby Blues®
Baby Blues®: Ten Years and Still in Diapers

BABY BLUES® 14 SCRAPBOOK

MOTHERHOOD
IS NOT FOR WIMPS

BY RICK KIRKMAN
AND JERRY SCOTT

Andrews McMeel
Publishing

Kansas City

Baby Blues is syndicated internationally by King Features Syndicate, Inc. For information, write King Features Syndicate, Inc., 235 East 45th Street, New York, New York 10017.

Motherhood Is Not For Wimps copyright © 2001 by Baby Blues Partnership. All rights reserved. Printed in the United States of America. No part of this book may be used or reproduced in any manner whatsoever without written permission except in the case of reprints in the context of reviews. For information, write Andrews McMeel Publishing, an Andrews McMeel Universal company, 4520 Main Street, Kansas City, Missouri 64111.

04 05 BAH 10 9 8 7 6 5

ISBN: 0-7407-1393-0

Library of Congress Catalog Card Number: 00-108457

Find *Baby Blues* on the Web at
www.babyblues.com

———— **ATTENTION: SCHOOLS AND BUSINESSES** ————

Andrews McMeel books are available at quantity discounts with bulk purchase for educational, business, or sales promotional use. For information, please write to: Special Sales Department, Andrews McMeel Publishing, 4520 Main Street, Kansas City, Missouri 64111.

To Jeff, Michele, and Olivia. Sano y salvo.
—J.S.

To Sukey with true love and admiration.
In remembrance of Irving Phillips . . . thank you for showing me the way.
—R.K.

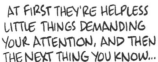

YAWN! I'M GOING TO BED.

OH, NO YOU'RE NOT, BUDDY.

GET DOWN HERE AND START ADDRESSING SOME OF THESE CHRISTMAS CARDS.

BUT IT'S ELEVEN-THIRTY!

SO?? IT'S ALSO DECEMBER THIRTEENTH, AND IF WE DON'T GET THESE OUT PRETTY SOON, OUR FRIENDS WILL TOTALLY FORGET WHO WE ARE!

SPEAKING OF THAT, WHO ARE **THESE** PEOPLE?

I DON'T KNOW, BUT THEY SEND US A CARD EVERY YEAR. JUST KEEP WRITING.

DID I HEAR DADDY COME IN?

YEAH... AND GUESS WHAT?

FWWWEEEEEET!

HE BOUGHT YOU WHISTLES?

AWWWW... WHO TOLD YOU?

MAY I BE EXCUSED?

NOT UNTIL YOU EAT MORE OF YOUR CASSEROLE.

I THINK I'LL GET SOME MORE CASSEROLE.

JUDGING BY YOUR WAISTLINE, I WONDER IF THAT'S A GOOD IDEA.

LUCKY DUCK.

LUCKY DUCK.

PLOP!

CLEANUP ON AISLE THREE!!

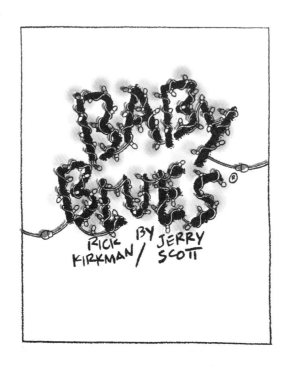

...ERE HE DROVE OUT OF SIGHT, "HAPPY CHRISTMAS TO ALL, AND TO ALL A GOOD NIGHT."

NOPE! NOT YET!

AWWWW!

WHAT'S HE **WAITING** FOR??

WELL, IT IS ONLY 5 PM...

KIRKMAN & SCOTT

WELL, THEY'RE FINALLY ASLEEP, ALL SNUG IN THEIR BEDS.

WHILE VISIONS OF SUGARPLUMS DANCE IN THEIR HEADS.

I DOUBT IT.

UNTIL SUGARPLUMS START BUYING SATURDAY MORNING TELEVISION COMMERCIAL TIME, THEY DON'T STAND A CHANCE!

KIRKMAN & SCOTT

HEY! WHEN DID THE KIDS GET IN BED WITH US?

I THINK IT WAS ABOUT THREE A.M.

THEY BOTH WOKE UP AND COULDN'T GO BACK TO SLEEP, SO I LET THEM CRAWL IN HERE WITH US.

KIRKMAN & SCOTT

WELL, SHALL WE GET UP AND START ENJOYING ALL THE BLESSINGS OF THE HOLIDAY?

I ALREADY AM.

17

20

I'M AFRAID THE BANK DOESN'T COUNT "A GOOD SENSE OF HUMOR" AS AN ASSET.

OBVIOUSLY, THE BANK HAS NEVER TRIED RAISING TWO KIDS ON ONE SALARY.

GAAACK!

LOANS

SCRUNCH

...AND I GOT THIS SCRAPE, AND BUMPED MY ELBOW, BENT THIS FINGER BACK AND GOT A SCRATCH ON THIS KNEE, BUT IT'S BETTER NOW...

WOW! SO THEN, YOU HAD A PRETTY ROUGH DAY AT SCHOOL, HUH?

NO.

THIS IS JUST FROM FIGHTING WITH HAMMIE IN THE CAR ON THE WAY HOME.

WE EITHER NEED A BIGGER VEHICLE, OR CAR SEATS WITH LIDS.

I THINK ZOE IS BECOMING A HYPOCHONDRIAC.

WHAT??

EVERY DAY SHE SPENDS THE FIRST TWENTY MINUTES AFTER SCHOOL DESCRIBING EVERY BUMP AND SCRAPE SHE GOT ON THE PLAY-GROUND IN EXCRUCIATING DETAIL.

SO...?

SO, MOST OF THESE SO-CALLED INJURIES DON'T EXIST! I THINK SHE'S MAKING THEM UP!

SO? LOTS OF KIDS FAKE AN INJURY TO GET ATTENTION ONCE IN A WHILE.

HERE'S WHAT WE SPENT ON BAND-AIDS LAST MONTH.

UH-OH.

PAPER CUT.

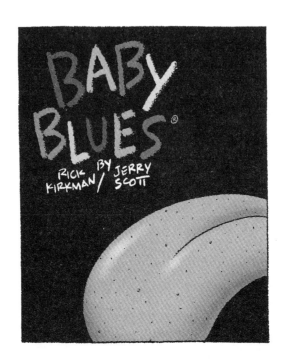

WHAT GOES AROUND, COMES AROUND... USUALLY A LITTLE TOO QUICKLY.

30

31

LOOK, HAMMIE! IF YOU DO THIS, YOU CAN CATCH SNOWFLAKES ON YOUR TONGUE!

BLECCH!

NOPE, THEY ONLY COME IN ONE FLAVOR.

WOO-HOOOO! IT'S THE WEEKEND! NO WORK!

NO SCHOOL!

YAY!

NOTHING TO DO BUT SIT AROUND AND RELAX!

AHHH!

AH!

MAN, AM I BORED.

ME, TOO.

Z

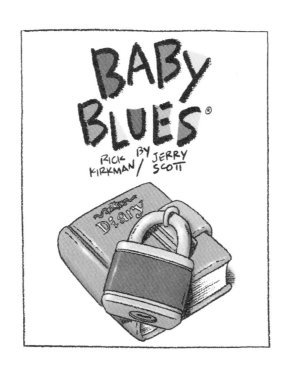

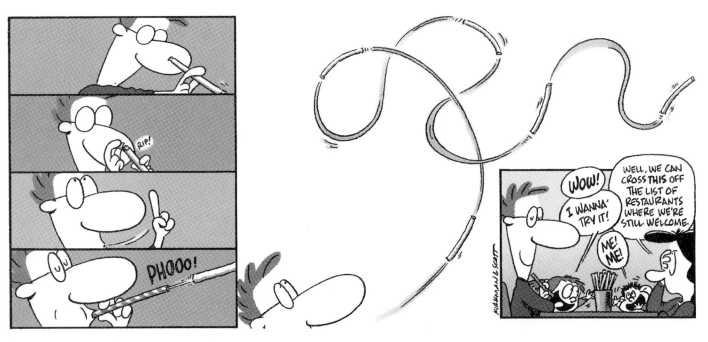

MOM! DAD! ONE OF THE CALLIPIDDERS MADE A COCOON!

HE SURE DID!

HOW ABOUT THAT!

AND AFTER THE CATERPILLAR IS FINISHED CHANGING INTO A BUTTERFLY, HE'LL COME OUT OF THE COCOON.

WHEN?

ACCORDING TO THIS, IN ABOUT A WEEK.

ISN'T NATURE AMAZING?

IF "AMAZING" MEANS SLOW, IT SURE IS!

TUESDAY

STILL IN THE COCOON!

WEDNESDAY

STILL IN THE COCOON.

THURSDAY

STILL IN THE COCOON.

FRIDAY

STILL IN THE COCOON?

NOT FOR LONG!

ZOE! HAMMIE! **LOOK!** A BUTTERFLY IS COMING OUT OF ITS COCOON!

ISN'T IT AMAZING HOW SOMETHING SO UGLY CAN TURN INTO SOMETHING SO BEAUTIFUL?

BUTTERFLY FARM

WHAT'S GOING ON?

WHAT DO YOU MEAN I NEED A COCOON?

38

HERE YOU GO, SWEETHEART.

WOW! HAMMIE IS EATING A LOT OF SOLID FOOD LATELY.

AT THIS RATE, IT WON'T BE LONG UNTIL YOU'RE FINISHED BREAST-FEEDING FOR GOOD!

HAPPY VALENTINE'S DAY, SWEETHEART.

A BAG FROM THE HARDWARE STORE? GEE, YOU SHOULDN'T HAVE.

I WONDER WHAT IT COULD BE! A POUND OF NAILS? NEW DRYWALL SCREWS? THAT CERTAIN SHEET OF SANDPAPER I'VE HAD MY EYE ON?

IT'S A TITANIUM DEADBOLT LOCK FOR YOUR BATHROOM DOOR.

THERE'S ROMANTIC, AND THEN THERE'S PRAGMATIC ROMANTIC...

IMAGINE TAKING A BUBBLE BATH WITHOUT HAVING TO NAIL THE DOOR SHUT...

HIDADDYGUESSWHATWEDIDINSCHOOLTODAYWEGOTTOSEEAMOVIEABOUTWHALESWHICHAREMAMMALSANDNOTFISHTHENWEWORKEDONMATHANDHEARDASTORYABOUTPOLARBEARSWELLGOTTAGOBYE!

ZOE IS SURE LEARNING A LOT OF THINGS IN KINDERGARTEN.

WHEN DO YOU SUPPOSE THEY'LL GET TO PUNCTUATION?

KIRKMAN & SCOTT

40

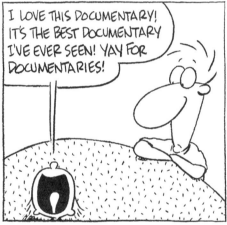

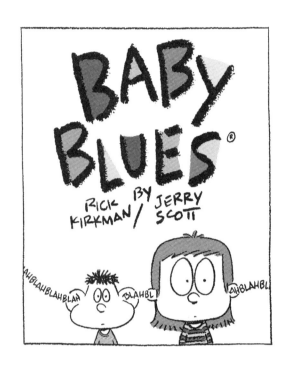

DON'T MOVE, DADDY! THERE'S A SPIDER ON YOU!

BAP! WAP! KONK! THWAP! BONK!

YOU HAVE TO BE CAREFUL... THOSE THINGS CAN HURT YOU!

SLURP! SLURP!

MMMM!

THIS SOUP IS GOOD!

M!

I'M GLAD YOU LIKE IT. IT'S CREAM OF BROCCOLI.

THERE'S NOTHING WORSE THAN FINDING OUT THAT YOU LIKE SOMETHING YOU HATE!

PTHOOEY!

HI, DAD.

UH, ZOE, MAY I ASK HOW MANY SWEATERS YOU'RE WEARING?

SIX.

YOU'RE WEARING SIX SWEATERS AT ONCE?

YEP.

IT WAS EITHER THAT, OR HANG THEM UP.

EENIE, MEENIE, MINEY, MOE! CATCH A TIGER BY HIS TOE! IF HE HOLLERS LET HIM GO!

MY-MOTHER-TOLD-ME-TO-PICK-THE-VERY-BEST-ONE-AND-IT-IS-THIS-ONE-OVER-HERE-BUT-MAYBE-NOT-BECAUSE-IT-MIGHT-BE-THIS-ONE-SO-I-DON'T-KNOW-WHICH-ONE-I-SHOULD-CHOOSE-BECAUSE-THEY-BOTH-ARE-GOOD-AND-I-LIKE...

IT LOOKS LIKE ZOE INHERITED HER DAD'S RED HAIR AND HIS DECISION-MAKING SKILLS, TOO.

WHADDYA THINK?... SHOULD I WEAR THE BROWN TIE, OR THE BROWNISH TIE?

45

Panel 1: OHMYGOSH! YOUR EYE IS ALL RED AND PUFFY, ZOE!

Panel 2: I WONDER IF IT COULD BE PINKEYE?

WHAT'S THAT?

BLINK! BLINK!

Panel 3: IT'S AN INFECTION OF THE EYE WE'LL HAVE TO BE CAREFUL BECAUSE IT'S VERY...

Panel 4: ...CONTAGIOUS.

BLINK! BLINK!

BLINK! BLINK!

Panel 5: IT'S CONJUNCTIVITIS, MRS. MacPHERSON.

Panel 6: JUST PUT THESE DROPS IN EACH EYE FOUR TIMES A DAY AND YOU SHOULDN'T HAVE ANY PROBLEM AT ALL.

Panel 7: YEP... NO-O-O-O-O PROBLEM AT ALL.

Panel 8: PINKEYE?? BOTH KIDS??

YEP. WE JUST GOT BACK FROM THE DOCTOR.

Panel 9: THEY EACH GET EYE DROPS FOUR TIMES A DAY FOR A WEEK.

WELL THAT DOESN'T SOUND TOO TOUGH.

Panel 10: NO. IN FACT, I'LL SHOW YOU HOW TO DO IT WHEN YOU GET HOME.

GREAT!

KIRKMAN & SCOTT

So this conjunctivitis thing is pretty contagious, huh?

Oh, yes, very.

It spreads like wildfire, so Zoe will need to stay home from school for a few days.

And we'll have to wash our hands a lot and sterilize anything the kids touch so we don't...

...catch it.

Too late.

:BLINK!:
:BLINK!:

AAAAAAGH! Now I've got pinkeye, too!

How can all four of us have it at once? It's not fair!

We look like a family of Popeye impersonators.

We yam what we yam.

YAAAAA! SQUIRT! SQUIRT! SQUIRT! SQUIRT! HYAAAA! SQUIRT! YAAAA! SQUIRT! SQUIRT!

You said to give the kids their eyedrops... you didn't say HOW.

 HOW ABOUT A LITTLE BITE OF YOUR ICE CREAM?

-OHH-KAYY...

SOMEBODY'S SHARING SKILLS NEED SOME WORK...

SOMEBODY'S LUCKY THE KIDS WERE WATCHING.

OH! HERE'S A GOOD ONE!

THIS IS A PICTURE OF ZOE TRYING TO EAT SPAGHETTI FOR THE FIRST TIME!

HA! HA! HA! HA! HA! HA! HA! HA! HA! HEE! HEE! HEE! HEE! HEE!

NOW SHOW US THE PICTURE OF THE FIRST TIME HAMMIE TRIED TO EAT SPAGHETTI.

UH...WE... UMM...WELL...

WE DON'T HAVE A SPAGHETTI PICTURE OF HAMMIE.

BUT YOU HAVE A FUNNY PICTURE OF ME EATING SPAGHETTI... WHY NOT HIM??

AFTER THE FIRST TIME, THE NOVELTY SORT OF WEARS OFF.

MUNCH   SLUUURP!
CRUNCH!
AHHH!

OKAY, MOMMY! ALL DONE!

YOU ATE ALL THOSE COOKIES? GOOD WORK!

THANKS!

WHAT ARE YOU WAITING FOR?

DESSERT!

HMMM...

DO THESE PANTS MAKE MY BUTT LOOK BIG?

ZIP!

YES.

:SIGH!: YOU'RE RIGHT.

WOW...I DIDN'T KNOW IT WAS POSSIBLE TO ANSWER "YES" TO THAT QUESTION AND LIVE!

I WOULDN'T TRY IT IF I WERE YOU.

MOM! HAMMIE IS TAKING ALL OF THE BLOCKS AND HE WON'T **SHARE!**

MOM! HAMMIE IS TAKING ALL THE COOKIES!

MOM! HAMMIE IS TAKING ALL OF THE BUBBLES!

≈SIGH!≈

MOM! HAMMIE IS BREATHING ALL THE AIR!

SNI-I-F-F!
SNI-I-I-F-F!
SNI-I-I-I-I-F-F!

YOUR TURN!

KIRKMAN & SCOTT

CAN I HAVE SOME MORE MILK, PLEASE?

SURE, SWEETIE.

OH— AND WHILE YOU'RE UP, WOULD YOU GET THE SALT?

OKAY.

DO WE HAVE ANY KETCHUP?

I'LL GET IT.

AND WHAT ABOUT PICKLES, TOO, HONEY?

OKAY.

CAN HAMMIE HAVE MORE CHEERIOS?

YES!

THERE! NOW ARE THERE ANY OTHER QUESTIONS BEFORE I SIT DOWN AND EAT **MY** DINNER?

WHAT'S FOR DESSERT?

KIRKMAN & SCOTT

WHAT'S THAT?

IT'S AN ULTRASOUND PICTURE OF YOU BEFORE YOU WERE BORN.

YOU MEAN WHILE I WAS STILL IN MOMMY'S TUMMY?

THAT'S RIGHT.

KIRKMAN & SCOTT

ZOE, WHAT ARE YOU DOING??

LOOKING FOR THE CAMERA.

YOU FIRST.

I'LL OPEN WITH A CRANKY BOSS.

I'LL SEE YOUR CRANKY BOSS AND RAISE YOU A PAIR OF BRATS.

OKAY... I'LL SEE YOUR BRATS, AND RAISE YOU A STAFF MEETING **AND** A COMPUTER OUTAGE.

I'LL SEE YOUR STAFF MEETING AND COMPUTER OUTAGE AND RAISE YOU ONE EARACHE, TWO RUNNY NOSES AND A RAINY DAY.

I FOLD.

THUNK!

I SHOULD KNOW BETTER THAN TO PLAY "LOUSY-DAY" POKER WITH A MOM.

PAY UP, SUCKER.

IF YOU SHAKE THE WATER OFF YOUR HANDS WHILE YOU'RE AT THE SINK, THE FLOOR DOESN'T GET ALL WET.

OHHHHHH.

KIRKMAN & SCOTT

WE FOUND A SHOW CALLED MTV!

CHANNEL LOCK! CHANNEL LOCK! CHANNEL LOCK!

KIRKMAN & SCOTT

70

MOMMY, IS THIS A WORD?

EEEP!

AH...UM...ER...UH...NO. IT'S NOT A WORD.

OH. OKAY.

SEE, I TOLD YOU THAT LETTERS CAN BE FUN!

ZOE AND HAMMIE HAVE BEEN FIGHTING SINCE THEY WOKE UP THIS MORNING, AND I'VE BEEN A TOTAL WITCH ALL DAY.

JUST WHEN I WAS ABOUT TO **REALLY** LOSE MY TEMPER, THEY BOTH CAME OVER AND GAVE ME A BIG HUG AND A KISS.

WELL, IT DOESN'T SOUND TO ME LIKE YOU WERE **THAT** MUCH OF A—

SO I DECIDED NOT TO COOK THEM AND EAT THEM FOR SUPPER AFTER ALL.

—WITCH.

COME HERE, HAMMIE...YOU HAVE A SMUDGE ON YOUR FACE.

NO!

COME HERE! I JUST WANT TO— HOLD STILL WHILE I— STOP PULLING AWAY SO I CAN—

NO! NO! NO! NO! NO! NO! NO!

WHUMP!

COME HERE...YOU HAVE A SMUDGE ON YOUR FACE.

THEY HAVE GRILLED CHEESY SANDWICH, CHICKY FINGERS 'N' FRIES, AND FISHY STICKS.

WHY DON'T YOU GET THE GRILLED CHEESE?

I DON'T LIKE GRILLED CHEESE

THEN GET THE CHICKY FINGERS.

OKAY, I'LL GET THAT.

GIVE US ONE CH—

NO, WAIT— I'LL HAVE THE FISHY STICKS.

MAKE THAT THE FISHY ST—

UNLESS YOU THINK I SHOULD HAVE THE CHICKY FINGERS.

LOOK, ZOE... YOU CAN HAVE ANYTHING YOU WANT. JUST MAKE UP YOUR MIND!

OKAY! OKAY! I'LL HAVE THE CHICKY FINGERS!

ARE YOU SURE?

YES!

SIGH! ONE CHICKY FINGERS AND A MILK, AND I'LL HAVE AN ICY TEA.

THAT'LL BE $2.87.

MMMM! CHICKY FINGERS! I LOVE CHICKY FINGERS! YUM! YUM! I CAN'T WAIT FOR MY CHICKY FINGERS!

ON SECOND THOUGHT, MAYBE I'LL HAVE THE GRILLED CHEESE.

KLUNK!

MOMMY, WOULD IT BE OKAY IF WE WENT OUTSIDE AND DREW ON THE PATIO WITH YOUR NEW LIPSTICK?

NO, IT WOULD NOT BE OKAY.

REALLY-NOT-OKAY, OR SORTA-NOT-OKAY?

REALLY NOT OKAY.

GO-TO-YOUR-ROOM-NOT-OKAY, OR NO-DESSERT-OR-TV-FOR-A-WEEK-NOT-OKAY?

I DON'T THINK I LIKE THE DIRECTION OF THIS CONVERSATION...

GO ASK THE LITTLE BOY IF HE WOULD LIKE TO PLAY WITH YOU, HAMMIE.

HIS NAME IS MATTHEW.

ALL YOU HAVE TO DO IS SAY, "HI, I'M HAMMIE. DO YOU WANT TO PLAY?"

TWUCK!

TWACTOR!

OR YOU COULD JUST SAY THAT...

HEAVY EQUIPMENT: THE UNIVERSAL LANGUAGE OF THE MALE.

MOMMY!

ATTACK OF THE KILLER DUST BUNNIES.

HOLD ME!

76

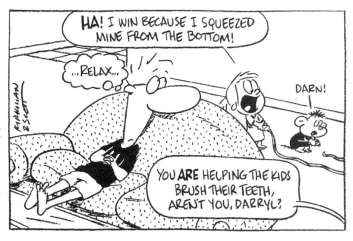

77

ZOE, WILL YOU HAND ME THAT PIECE OF PAPER THERE ON THE GROUND?

I'LL TAKE YOUR POPSICLE WRAPPERS, TOO.

AND WHEN YOU'RE FINISHED, BE SURE TO BRING ME THE POPSICLE STICKS AND YOUR NAPKINS, TOO, OKAY?

I WONDER WHY PARENTS LIKE GARBAGE SO MUCH?

OF COURSE...

...IT'S TIME TO DO THE DISHES, TIME TO WASH A LOAD OF CLOTHES, TIME TO BATHE THE KIDS, TIME TO GO GROCERY SHOPPING, TIME TO BALANCE THE CHECKBOOK, TIME TO WASH THE CAR, TIME TO VACUUM THE HOUSE...

NEVER ASK A BUSY MOM IF SHE KNOWS WHAT TIME IT IS.

TIME FOR EVERYTHING BUT ME!

MOMMY, CAN I HAVE AN ICE-CREAM BAR?

SURE.

UH-OH...THERE'S ONLY ONE LEFT.

I'LL JUST CUT IT IN HALF IN CASE HAMMIE WANTS SOME WHEN HE WAKES UP FROM HIS NAP.

ONLY MY LITTLE BROTHER COULD RUIN A GOOD TIME EVEN WHILE HE'S ASLEEP!

I DON'T KNOW WHAT TO PAINT.

PAINT A COWBOY.

AAAGH! THIS IS A TERRIBLE COWBOY!

IT'S BAD! IT'S STUPID! IT'S THE WORST PICTURE I EVER PAINTED AND IT'S ALL YOUR FAULT!

RIP!

SPLAT!

NOW WHAT SHOULD I PAINT?

ANYTHING BUT A COWBOY.

TODAY A KID NAMED MATTHEW SAID THAT HIS MOMMY IS PRETTIER THAN MY MOMMY.

AND WHAT DID YOU SAY?

I SAID SHE IS NOT, AND HE SAID SHE IS, TOO.

AND I SAID, IS NOT, AND HE SAID, IS, TOO, AND I SAID, IS NOT, AND HE SAID, IS, TOO, AND I SAID, IS NOT, AND PUNCHED HIM IN THE STOMACH.

I LIKE TO KEEP MY ARGUMENTS SHORT.

WHERE IS THE MIDDLE OF NOWHERE? WHO INVENTED TOOTHPASTE? WHAT'S CARPET MADE OF? HOW DOES SOUND COME OUT OF THE RADIO? DO FISH SMILE? HOW MANY PAGES IN A BOOK? WHY DON'T GORILLAS WEAR JEWELRY?

WHAT DOES THE "T" IN T-SHIRT STAND FOR? HOW DO THEY GET THE LEAD INTO PENCILS? WHERE DOES GUM COME FROM? IF YOU WEAR A SWEATER, DO YOU HAVE TO SWEAT? IS A COMPUTER SMARTER THAN A TELEPHONE? DO CHICKENS SING?

SUMMER FOR WOMEN

TIME TO GET IN SHAPE FOR THE OL' SWIMSUIT!

SUMMER FOR MEN

TIME TO BUY A BIGGER SWIMSUIT!

SUMMER FOR KIDS

WHY DO WE HAVE TO WEAR SWIMSUITS?

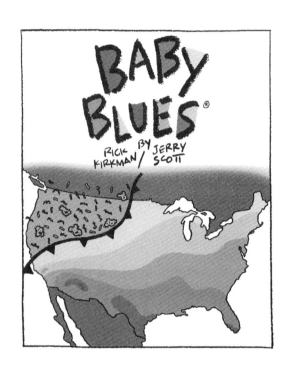

88

89

90

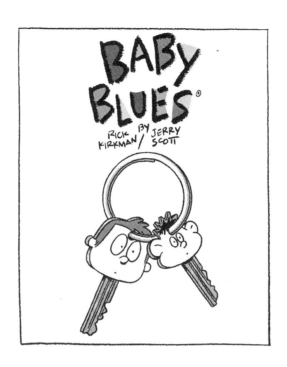

OH! THAT'S SO CUTE! I SHOULD MAKE A NOTE IN HAMMIE'S BABY BOOK!

I MEAN, I **WOULD** IF I COULD REMEMBER WHERE I PUT IT. AND IF I COULD FIND A PEN. AND IF THAT PEN HAD ANY INK IN IT. AND IF I HAD THIRTY UNINTERRUPTED SECONDS TO PUT TOGETHER A COHERENT SENTENCE...

¿SIGH!¿ THE PAGES OF A SECOND CHILD'S BABY BOOK ARE FILLED WITH GOOD INTENTIONS.

KIRKMAN & SCOTT

ZOE! HAMMIE! WASH YOUR HANDS BEFORE DINNER!

AND USE SOAP THIS TIME!

NOW SIT UP STRAIGHT AND EAT YOUR VEGETABLES!

DON'T TALK WITH YOUR MOUTH FULL!

USE YOUR NAPKIN!

KIRKMAN & SCOTT

THERE YOU GO, MOM. NOW YOU CAN TAKE THE REST OF THE NIGHT OFF.

VERY FUNNY.

¿SNICKER!¿

♫ I SEE LONDON! I SEE FRANCE! I SEE HAMMIE'S UNDERPANTS! ♫

HA! HA! HA! HA! HA! HA! HA! HA! HA! HA!

OKAY.

THAT SONG IS A LOT FUNNIER IF THE PERSON YOU'RE SINGING ABOUT ISN'T WALKING AROUND IN A DIAPER.

KIRKMAN & SCOTT

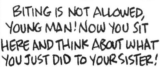

95

BABY BLUES®

RICK KIRKMAN / BY JERRY SCOTT

HAPPY FATHER'S DAY!

WOW! WHAT'S ALL THIS?

WELL, WE MADE YOU SOME COLD TOAST AND WEAK COFFEE.

OH, GOODIE.

AND AFTER YOU OPEN YOUR PRESENTS, WE'RE GOING TO DISAPPEAR FOR A WHILE, LEAVING YOU TO CLEAN UP THE INCREDIBLE MESS WE LEFT IN THE KITCHEN.

HUH?

THEN WE'RE GOING TO PIN A HUGE UGLY FLOWER ON YOUR SHIRT AND TAKE YOU OUT TO BRUNCH AT A BIG, IMPERSONAL HOTEL RESTAURANT WHERE THEY SERVE VATS OF RUNNY SCRAMBLED EGGS AND UNDERCOOKED BACON THAT TASTE LIKE THEY WERE PREPARED IN A PRISON KITCHEN, AND, OF COURSE, THEY'LL HAVE CHAMPAGNE BY THE PITCHER.

THIS IS BEGINNING TO SOUND A LOT LIKE WHAT WE DID FOR MOTHER'S DAY...

♪TURNABOUT IS FAIR PLAY!♪

GET DRESSED! LET'S GO!

YAY!

KIRKMAN & SCOTT

98

...ROSE COSSETTE...CHRIS HOLLANDER...

DON'T BE SHY, ZOE, JUST WALK RIGHT UP THERE AND GET YOUR DIPLOMA!

...CHELLE JOHANSEN...QUINN LINCOLN...

DON'T BE SHY...DON'T BE SHY... DON'T BE SHY...

...ZOE MacPHERSON...

HI MOMMY! HI DADDY!

HEY, AT LEAST SHE WASN'T SHY...

THIS IS GOING TO BE COOL! I TOLD ZOE TO THROW HER CAP INTO THE AIR LIKE THE MIDSHIPMEN AT ANNAPOLIS.

LADIES AND GENTLEMEN, I GIVE YOU THE KINDERGARTEN GRADUATING CLASS OF 2000!

THERE IT GOES!

OW! HEY! ZOE THREW HER HAT AT ME!

WAAAAA! MOMMY!

ZOE MacPHERSON WILL NOW STAY AFTER THE CEREMONY TO HELP PICK UP TRASH.

THANKS A LOT, DAD!

WELL, IT'S COOL WHEN THE MIDSHIPMEN DO IT...

SO, ARE YOU EXCITED ABOUT GRADUATING FROM KINDERGARTEN, ZOE?

UH-HUH.

I WAS GETTING TIRED OF ALL THE THINGS WE HAD TO DO, LIKE LISTENING TO THE TEACHER, DOING HOMEWORK AND SITTING STILL.

I CAN'T WAIT TO START FIRST GRADE SO I CAN TAKE IT EASY FOR A CHANGE.

YEAH. THEN AFTER YOU GROW UP, GET A JOB AND START A FAMILY, LIFE'S REALLY A BREEZE!

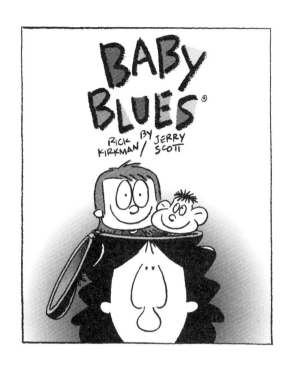

NOW REMEMBER WHAT I SAID... YOU CAN PICK OUT **ONE** VIDEO TO RENT.

THAT MEANS THAT YOU TWO ARE GOING TO HAVE TO COOPERATE AND CHOOSE **ONE** MOVIE THAT YOU **BOTH** WANT TO SEE.

I'M NOT WALKING OUT OF HERE WITH A WHOLE STACK OF MOVIES LIKE THE LAST TIME!

:SIGH!:

RENT IT NOW, KEEP IT FOR 3 DAYS!

LET'S GET ONE THING STRAIGHT... I AM **NOT** BUYING YOU ANY CANDY IN HERE.

OKAY.

I MEAN IT.

I KNOW.

WE'RE JUST HERE TO PICK UP SOME SALAD DRESSING AND CHEESE. THAT'S ALL. GOT IT?

GOT IT.

I DON'T KNOW WHICH IS WORSE... SUSPECTING THAT YOU'RE A PUSHOVER, OR PROVING IT BEYOND THE SHADOW OF A DOUBT.

SMACK! SMACK!

MMM!

DARRYL, I ASK YOU TO TAKE THE KIDS TO RENT A MOVIE, AND YOU COME BACK WITH **SEVEN** OF THEM!

THEN I SEND YOU TO THE STORE WITH THEM TO BUY SALAD DRESSING AND YOU COME BACK WITH A HUGE BAG OF CANDY AND A LICORICE WHIP!

I DON'T THINK YOU **CAN** SAY "**NO**" TO THE KIDS!

I CAN SO!

LATER... TOYCO

CAN WE GO HOME AND SHOW MOMMY WHAT YOU BOUGHT US THIS TIME?

NO.

108

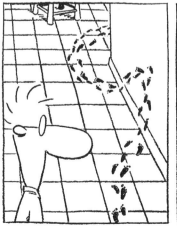

DING-A-LING-A-LING ♪♫
OH NO.

POW!

DARRYL! GO TELL THE KIDS THAT THE ICE CREAM TRUCK IS ON OUR STREET!
THEY KNOW.
KIRKMAN & SCOTT

COME ON, DADDY! HURRY UP!
OKAY! OKAY! I'M COMING!
HUWWY!
KIRKMAN & SCOTT

THE ICE CREAM TRUCK STOPPING ON OUR STREET... DADS WALKING THEIR KIDS OUT TO THE SIDEWALK... IT'S JUST LIKE WHEN I WAS A KID.

THAT'LL BE $12.75.
...ONLY DIFFERENT.
CAUTION: CHILDREN AROUND

CHA-CHING!
CAUTION: CHILDREN

AAAGGHH!
PLOP!

THAT'S OKAY... I'LL JUST BLOW IT OFF! ≋PHOO! PHOO!≋ THERE! GOOD AS NEW!

WHAT ABOUT THE GERMS?
AT $4.25 PER ICE CREAM BAR, GERMS DON'T STICK.
KIRKMAN & SCOTT

DARRYL, HAMMIE WOKE UP FROM HIS NAP, AND HE WANTS TO PLAY IN THE SWIMMING POOL.

OKAY, I'LL WATCH HIM.

BRRRMM-CHU-KNK!

HIS SWIMMING TRUNKS ARE IN THE BATHROOM ON THE TOWEL RACK!

I FOUND THEM!

DON'T FORGET TO TAKE HIS DIAPER OFF FIRST!

DID IT!

BE SURE TO PUT SUNSCREEN ON HIM.

DONE!

ZIP!

TRIP!

WHUMP!

OH, AND SINCE I JUST FINISHED MOWING THE LAWN, LET THE SUNSCREEN DRY BEFORE YOU LET HIM OUT.

OOPS.

P.THOO!

BABY BLUES
RICK KIRKMAN / BY JERRY SCOTT

DON'T LOOK NOW, BUT YOU'VE **GOT** TO SEE THAT FAMILY OVER THERE!

WHERE?

I JUST GOT A GLIMPSE OF THEM, BUT TALK ABOUT YOUR SMALL-TOWN GOOBERS!

SHHHH! THEY'LL HEAR YOU!

TO 6 PM

THE GUY IS PROBABLY ABOUT MY AGE, BUT HE LOOKS LIKE HE HASN'T EXERCISED IN ABOUT FIVE YEARS...

YEAH?

AND THE WIFE ISN'T MUCH BETTER! SHE HAS BAGS UNDER HER EYES THAT WOULDN'T QUALIFY AS CARRY-ON LUGGAGE, AND A HAIRSTYLE THAT WENT OUT IN THE EIGHTIES!

REALLY?

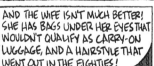

OH! AND TO COMPLETE THE ENSEMBLE, THEY'RE DRAGGING A COUPLE OF MESSY, SNOT-NOSED KIDS ALONG IN A WAGON!

A WAGON??

I THINK I'M GOING TO CRY.

CAN YOU SAY "HI" TO BUNNY, ZOE?

HI. CAN BOGART PLAY TODAY?

BOGART IS AT HIS LESSONS TODAY, SWEETHEART.

HE HAS A VIOLA LESSON AT 9, TENNIS AT 10, HORSE-BACK RIDING AT 12:30 AND FRENCH CLASS AT 2.

THEIR MINDS ARE LIKE LITTLE SPONGES FOR KNOWLEDGE, AREN'T THEY?

LOOK WHAT MY DADDY IS TEACHING ME TO DO!

FWEET! FWEET!

SO, ARE YOU HOPING FOR A BOY OR A GIRL THIS TIME, BUNNY?

I WANT ANOTHER BOY.

I JUST HAD ALL OF BOGART'S BABY CLOTHES CLEANED, I'VE RE-DONE THE NURSERY IN A COWBOY MOTIF, AND EVEN PICKED OUT A BOY'S NAME.

BUT WHAT IF IT'S A GIRL?

IT WOULDN'T DARE!

ONCE A CONTROL FREAK, ALWAYS A CONTROL FREAK.

WHY WAS BUNNY OVER HERE?

TO TELL ME SOME NEWS.

IT LOOKS LIKE BOGART IS GOING TO GET A NEW LITTLE BROTHER.

HE IS?? I WANT A NEW LITTLE BROTHER, TOO!

YOU HAVE A LITTLE BROTHER, ZOE.

BUT I WANT A NEW ONE!

THAT ONE'S USED!

126

I JUST LOVE TALKING WITH YOLANDA!

WE COVERED EVERYTHING TONIGHT! RELATIVES, HOUSES, POLITICS, FURNITURE, KIDS, NEIGHBORS, RELIGION, MONEY, MARRIAGE... THE WORKS!

WHAT DID YOU AND MIKE TALK ABOUT?

BARBECUE.